what's next 〉〉

2020 EDITION

Generis®   **DAVE TRAVIS**
with Rob Suggs

This book is published by Generis Partners LLC.
For more information about Generis,
visit www.generis.com

Printed and Kindle versions are available at
www.amazon.com

Foreword

At Generis, our heartbeat is the local church—not the church as a doctrine. Not the church as an abstract, theological idea. We're passionate about living, breathing churches on the streets, in service, tending to genuine, soul-deep needs.

Which isn't to say we look through rose-tinted glasses. Actually, we work with leaders on the front lines of battle, where the wounds are; where emotions run high; where there can be discouragement. We know the issues that pastors and boards are facing today, and those issues are deadly serious.

Today, if you don't possess a clear understanding of the stakes, you're unlikely to last in ministry. Quite frankly, the church is under fire from more than one direction. Some of our most basic beliefs are being challenged seriously for the first time.

One statement we make in this book is that our leaders can't hide from the tougher issues—the nature of marriage, just to mention one of many. Silence is not an option. Even at the risk of losing donors, we must be clear with the world about who we are, what we believe, and why. Millennials in particular—the generation we can't fail to reach—won't allow our silence. To repurpose Paul's words to Timothy, we must be prepared to give an answer to anyone who asks.

Generis takes no stance on what your particular answer should be. We're not in the business of sorting out theological particularities, because we know you can do that very well for yourself. We simply exhort you to be clear and positive as you proclaim the gospel to a generation that demands transparency and accountability.

The church has always resisted, then weathered, then leveraged change. Today is no different. This is one of those periods when we feel the ground shifting beneath our feet, the tectonic plates clashing. We urge you not to resist change, but to meet it squarely; to greet it as your best opportunity to be part of God doing something new and thrilling. The temptation will always be to retreat into the nostalgia of the good old days, with the "comfortable crowd," where very temporary shelter is found. It can't last, and the risk is diminished effectiveness as God's rescue workers in a turbulent world.

This is why, at Generis, our work is in developing high-capacity, high-energy leaders. We believe these leaders won't simply survive—they'll fight the battle in such a way as to win, and they'll write the next chapter in the two-thousand-year story of a persevering, victorious church.

People will follow leaders of that type. They'll give generously to the clear, compelling cause those leaders articulate. And out of their midst will come the leaders of our children's and grandchildren's generations, still weathering change, still showing how God's love prevails regardless of the intensity of the storm.

That, we believe, is what's next. God doing a new thing is always what's next—though, sure, there are details, too. Dave Travis lays those out for you in the following chapters. We believe you'll be challenged and inspired by these pages.

Read these ideas, wrestle with them, and then let us know what we at Generis can do to help you prevail.

Partnering with you,

Jim Sheppard
CEO & Principal, Generis
Brad Leeper
President & Principal, Generis

The Future, Again

I talk to senior pastors. Lots of them.

These are men and women who lead congregations of all kinds; nearly every leadership model imaginable. Each congregation is a story all its own anyway—no two are quite alike.

Yet in nearly every case, our conversations follow a similar pattern.

First come the pleasantries. Ice is broken. Smiles are exchanged. Coffee is sipped.

Then I ask, "So what's happening here?" We're ready for an update of the leader's progress in ministry. Together we review the recent highlights.

It's after that when we get to the real question. My friend looks at me and asks, "What's next for our church?"

It's the issue at hand, the real reason we're talking. Like everyone else trying to keep moving through turbulent waters, churches must have at least some idea of what lies ahead and how to prepare for it.

In 2012, I decided to create a snapshot of that moment's answer, and offer it in booklet form. With a mastery of the obvious, I entitled it, *What's Next?*

The work's audience was the clientele of Leadership Network. I felt we were hearing the question with even deeper urgency, and I wanted to issue a call for leaders to gather their boards and leader-groups and plan more deeply and wisely.

What's Next? was well-received among its narrower clientele—but it also resonated with a wider audience. Because of the interest and questions sparked by the booklet, I followed up with a brief, private update for our clients the next year.

Somehow, seven years have moved past us in a headlong, tumultuous rush. Yesterday's "down the road" is today's rear-view mirror. Brand new hills and horizons fill the windshield now, and they're just as daunting as ever. It's time to look ahead and ask the next set of questions, always with a pragmatic, rolled-up-sleeves mindset.

The subtext remains, *What should our leadership group be doing right this moment?*

Background and Biases

Maybe you and I haven't talked in the past. What you're wondering is, who is this writer to offer a guided tour of my future?

What, if anything, is this guy's prophetic portfolio?

It's a fair question.

For three decades, I've served on platforms providing ministry to multiple churches. Leadership Network has been my vocational home for the past 25 years, and I've mostly been in conversation with the largest churches in America.

Yet I've always had an ear to the ground for churches of other sizes. I've kept in touch with church planters, church-planting networks, and denominational leadership. I've stayed up to date with the church scene as a whole.

Early in my career, I was an associate pastor; then I was elected as the administrative and missions leader for a local denominational region in the late 1980s. I spent time "on the ground" with the daily cares of churches and missions.

In 1995, I began serving Leadership Network in many roles. Though intermittently I continued serving a dozen churches, at different times, as an interim pastor, I'm not ordained as one. I continue as a lay deacon and remain a lay servant to the church.

For my first 15 years of association with Leadership Network, I was blessed to lead the team of directors, staff, and consultants. They provided me with eyes and ears across the U. S., Canada, and even Europe, with a focus on the most innovative churches. Each year, we went deep with as many as 300 leaders from the front line. We kept in touch on the phone, through email and text, and during private visits.

My mentors, besides my parents, pastors, and colleagues, include Lyle Schaller. We met while I was in seminary, then continued our friendship through hosting some events together, as well as through his writings, his training sessions, and my frequent visits to his home. It was Dr. Schaller who recommended me to Leadership Network.

I stand on the shoulders of two other giants of our field. Peter Drucker, the legendary management expert, conducted events for Leadership Network; and again, I enjoyed visits to his home. These were arranged by Bob Buford, one of the Leadership Network founders and my mentor for the last 27 years of his life.

Bob's passing in the spring of 2018 came as I was transitioning from the CEO role to a new role at Leadership Network as Senior Consultant.

Now I've joined with Generis, the giving and guidance specialists, to help create a new area focused on senior leadership, strategy, and board development.

I bring with me my wide network of colleagues and alumni staff—adding to it a new set of listening posts with the Generis team, more than 40 professionals serving churches across the nation. Our clients include evangelicals, mainliners, charismatic, and Pentecostal followers of Jesus.

In addition, I now draw on a wider network of researchers, academics, and think tank fellows, helping me test ideas from other fields in churches.

But in one field, I know much less than you— your own church; your ministry outpost.

You're the one who is living out that particular story, along with its backstory and its special uniqueness. I bring news from the wider world, the culture-driven trends shaping the landscape. But you know the specifics of your location. Between us, we can create a plan that will bring the right chemistry for the looming challenges.

Two decades of listening have kept me current in the research and findings of church work and the culture at large. Demographic changes, media, tech, pop culture, politics, and all kinds of other factors have helped shape these views. More than 100 books a year came across my desk, in addition to my own intentional purchases.

That's a picture of the overall data. But don't worry! In this book, you won't find extensive notes or annotations or "info dumps." No master's thesis work here. This is a memo for busy workers in the field, the kind of laborers who must batten down the hatches before the storm sets in. This is a book about urgency, next steps, and quick response strategy.

Why Tomorrow Matters Today

Someone said the problem with the Christian life is it's so daily. And every Church leader knows that weekends are far too weekly. Nothing is more insistent than time.

Next weekend is never more than a few days away, and for churches, these mean the busy-ness of multiple gatherings: worship services, kids ministries, youth activities, and nearly everything that's make or break for us.

The nature of the beast is that leaders always have their hands full with the current activity. And today, these events can't be stale or "same-y." Creativity and freshness are demanded.

It can be tiring. Churches may put together annual plans and cast visions and work to stay on task. And that's all fine and good. Still, every other year, you need to stop the world from spinning and climb off to catch your breath and see the big picture.

You need time to look way down the road—farther than next weekend or the weekend after that—and see what's coming, and what's bigger even than the next weekly emphasis. It's less micro and more macro. This may not mean changing anything now set in stone on the church calendar, but it's time to begin thinking about what's *next*, so that future planning can be shaped accordingly—so that today's stuff can begin with the end in mind.

This booklet is written with that kind of foresight on the agenda. It should spur your thinking given the coming trends and influences we see coming, so that you can ask, *What does this mean for us? How can we avoid being unsettled and ambushed, and instead capitalize on these changes toward fruitful ministry, as winning leaders do?*

As your team reads this booklet together, you may be stimulated and even encouraged by the brainstorming sessions that result. That's the plan.

And like perennial movers and shakers, you'll find that change isn't the enemy at all; it's the portal through which God reaches as he uses us to do a new thing.

1. Is Demography Destiny?

The idea of demographics has fully arrived in the public domain. It's no longer the shop talk of sociologists and marketing professionals. It's almost a household word.

We all know that people come in groups—by birth year, by educational qualifications, by gender and geography, by income bracket and racial identity. These descriptions are predictive of a great many things, including ministry opportunity.

American history can be studied as an evolution of demographic patterns. For example, the "baby boomers," that most famed of all generation groups, created a shift in American culture across the fields of education, politics, religion, financial services, employment, family formation, and just about everything else. They even got us talking about demographics and generations.

When we wish to speak in simple terms, we can look through the lens of demography: birth year, gender, location, and the like. We can also study attitude shifts—prevalent opinions on various issues. Those are all fairly easily measurable. Marketers look deeply into the numbers and notions. But most telling of all is the actual *behavioral* information. That's where we find out what people actually *do* in relation to predictive data.

Smart leaders listen to the number crunchers. They access these bundles of information as tools for creatively addressing people in sharing the gospel and growing the faith.

So we've come to a consensus that demography tells us a lot about our world. But is it destiny?

Religious Leaders Are Smarter Than You Think

American religious practitioners have paid reasonably good attention to the research. They have a 200-year history of adapting to landscape changes and adapting their churches to address their times and challenges wisely.

The European church has lagged a bit in comparison; other continents have adapted more along the American pattern of flexibility. In places where a "free market" of business and ideas is available, the church has enjoyed more success in fluidly adapting to the times.

When I entered the ministry in the early 1980s, many of these understandings were being applied to the gospel task at hand. A whole new field arose in which Christian leadership addressed demographic data more attentively. Forward thinkers helped pastors and leaders understand that if the "new wine" of the gospel is eternal and unchanging, someone needs to be watching the wineskins for leakage.

This led to powerful movements in American Christendom. The example that comes most quickly to mind is the term *seeker-sensitive*. The idea was, "Our people have changed. They're less interested in older forms of worship, and it's time to refit the old truth in a modern, more casual manner."

There was a specific generational target—baby boomers—and attention to "felt need" preaching and ministry. It was a comprehensive makeover of the church at virtually every level other than theology. Programs, outreach, and even architecture reflected a sensitivity to an audience that had been falling away.

Yet new wineskins become old ones after a while. The children and even the grandchildren of the boomers must be reached. "Attractional" ministry itself is now in question, and demographic data reads differently than it did 25 to 30 years ago.

As always, a fresh look and careful thought are needed. But where do we start? How much change can the church navigate without losing its identity?

As always, the first draft of a new approach is uncomfortable. It looks foreign, unwieldy, and raises questions in terms of how much change is acceptable change. We must learn to live within that tension, as we've done ever since Paul met with the Jerusalem church and spoke of a wider world.

Local and National

Much of the above is stipulated with our audience; if you didn't agree that leadership models must adapt to changing times, you wouldn't have picked up this booklet. It's the issues themselves—the nature of the wineskins—we're most eager to discuss.

Before leaning into some of those specifics, however, it's worth being reminded that we don't deal with a homogeneous world. The context is always local. There are general understandings of contemporary culture writ large, but your neighborhood realities are ultimately unique. Most congregations— even multisite ones—have defined their context in slices of landscape that may be as small as a two-mile radius or as large as a metropolitan region.

That's a reality to keep in mind: the particular in relation to the general. Even so, the national trends discussed here must be reckoned with, for they're the backdrop, the larger context of your church's story.

Good leaders have a sense of the local and the national, just as a sports fan knows his or her team as well as the league it plays in. Leaders see waves of change that may not have arrived in our neighborhood yet, but are surely coming. They're conversant with the national trend, but they adapt it based on their own particularities. Dual focus is the key.

Example: Many congregations are planted in smaller cities in more exurban areas, while others exist in the suburbs of a major metropolitan area. The rhythms of life are different in these two locales, and the church's response will be different.

What follows are the major developments on their way—trends that need to be well considered in advance by prepared leaders. The particulars of your response, and how you address the micro-trends of your local situation, are questions beyond our scope here. But the back of this booklet offers suggestions of how I may be of service to you at your local level.

Why do groups of people respond to the gospel? What draws them inside the doors of the church or the reach of one of its ministries? How can people be encouraged to linger and lean into spiritual growth?

The answers rise, in part, from how people have been raised; what their family lives are like; how their careers influence their actions; the molding of their education. And there are many other factors. There's a lot to consider when we look into the faces of our people, whom Jesus saw as "sheep without a shepherd." We feel compassion. We want to offer them the greatest gift imaginable. But we must make the right approach, because we may not get another shot.

Jesus spoke of the kinds of soil that determine whether the seed takes root. Our study is ultimately about testing the ground, understanding the richness of the earth where our seeds are planted, and deciding how to make the soil as fertile as possible. The seeds we have are God-made; they're perfect, so it's the quality of that topsoil that makes all the difference. Our data is the best chance for evaluating it.

Generational theory remains a popular shorthand for organizing our thoughts on those faces that surround us—Boomers, Gen-X, Millennials. The categories are imperfect, of course, but they provide us a useful place to start.

A GenXact Science

Sometimes the best-laid plans go awry, as the poet said.

We do our best to focus on the next generation coming along, and we use all the data before us to figure out what to expect. But we can get it wrong.

In 1995, I joined Leadership Network. The baby boomer approaches to churches were coming into their own, but forward-thinkers already had an eye on their Generation X children and emerging adults—roughly those born between 1965 and 1981. In order to address those concerns, Leadership Network and others held extensive discussions. We convened practitioners and experts to examine the demographics and make adjustments.

In short, most of the predictions I heard were wrong.

Instead of the expected rejection of all things boomer and prior, nuanced approaches were developed.

Instead of the massification and entrenchment of churches springing up within churches, the direction was outward: new venues and sites.

Disproving the warnings about a whole generation of slackers and clerks, a new entrepreneurial generation emerged.

And instead of the dire pronouncements of the next wave falling away from faith, we saw multiple new leaders emerge who were more traditional and conservative in their theological positions than many of their parents.

As wilderness scouts of the trail ahead, we got the whole landscape wrong. What did we miss? Better question, what can we learn from our misadventure?

We're wrong to confuse continuity and discontinuity—how much the pathways will remain constant, and how much they'll diverge. Proclaiming massive discontinuity makes for bold pronouncements, but it often proves wrong, at least for a certain time. Then it may come true after all.

For example, the predictors of early 90s American religion missed the rapid rise of neo-Reformed and other similar movements among younger religious leaders. What played out was a trend of young church leaders who were more traditional in their theology than their forebears, while being highly adaptable in congregational practice.

Future prediction is more an art than a science. As we speak of what's next, we must do so with the humility of remembering that only God knows exactly how it will all play out. Who could foresee the current political environment? Who knew the War Against Terror was coming before 9/11? How about the financial crisis of a decade ago?

All of these forces shape the church along with everything else. In other words, X-factors help make this an inXact science.

Millennials to the Max

We can all agree we've reached "peak millennial" status in our generation-watching. Everyone seems to be an expert on this age group. But how much do we really know about them?

Let's set some parameters. Those born between 1981 and 1996 qualify, so that the youngest are in their early twenties, the oldest actually approaching 40.

In leadership planning, we tend to look to those in the generation that is coming of age in terms of marriage and childbearing. These are also the years when careers begin, houses are bought, and life patterns established. So at this moment in time, millennials should be of supreme interest to church leaders.

Here are some snapshots of the millennial generation, also known as GenY.

1. As of 2019, they're expected to overtake the boomers as America's largest generational group. Their numbers will eclipse 73 million as the boomers fall below that level. How can their numbers climb when we're past their birth era? Immigration patterns. Almost one in three Americans is a millennial.

2. They're the most racially diverse generation. Depending upon the birth year chosen, millennials average about 45 percent non-white. We can expect this trend to continue into the generation that follows as racial diversity becomes a given in American life. By way of comparison, the young adults of 1980—those in the same age ranges—were 78 percent white/Anglo. Together, millennials and GenZ make up 37 percent of the American electorate in the next presidential election, 2020.

3. After Anglo, Hispanic is the second largest grouping among the millennials. Hispanic is a broad and often problematic term, but the census bureau uses it to capture a region of family origin. Sometimes the term Latino is also used, but confusion again ensues. Adding to the controversy, many in this category avoid the term after a certain period of time. Still, the census counts just over 20 percent in this

category. Black/African American comes in at 14 percent, Asians at 6 percent.

4. Homes headed by millennials have higher incomes than previous generations of those age designations. This goes against the grain of common assumptions, but the fact is, more women are in the workplace in this age group, and those women have better, higher-earning jobs than the women who preceded them.

5. Marriage and family dynamics: These represent the greatest changes. More than one million millennials are becoming moms for the first time each year with 17 to 19 million already in that category. While there's a much-ballyhooed trend toward delaying child bearing, most in this age group desire marriage and family in the same ways that prior generations did. In fact, research suggests that millennials have an even stronger desire to excel at parenting than the boomers had.

6. As for marriage, keep in mind we track generations at common milestones. At present, approximately 57 percent of millennials have never married. At the same point in their lives 43 percent of GenXers had never married; only 33 percent of boomers. This points to a delay

and deferral of marriage, but not necessarily a rejection. Thirty-seven percent of millennials are now married, compared to a figure of 56 percent of boomers at similar stages of life in the past. This is the very kind of factor that impacts churches significantly.

7. Millennials have the highest percentage of households in poverty. It's only a slight difference, but it points to the skewing of economics as seen by this generation. Based on the fact that many more are minorities with traditionally lower incomes and wealth in prior generations, again we see the generational impact.

8. Millennials are more likely than other generations to rent their homes. Home ownership in America has been stable for about 30 years, with only slight variations, depending on economic downturns. As millennials advance in age, we find that 37 percent are likely to own their own homes, compared to 45 percent of Xers and boomers at the comparable ages. Some of this is economic and related to diversity issues; some is all about location— where they live and where they desire to work. This trend is most closely related to urban and metro situations.

9. They're actually less mobile when it comes to moving from home to home. Compared to the previous generations at similar ages, millennials are less likely to migrate. This only covers those out of prime college years in all cases.

10. They're better educated and more tied to academic settings than previous generations. They have more school time, more degrees, and a generally higher level of book-learning.

Those factors should get the conversation started. There are many other cultural factors at play that we haven't even addressed. Instead, let's simply look at a few of the implications through simple examples. These will help us point out changes to how we've seen ministry in the past.

I give this kind of overview to groups across the country. I always explain how past generations of churches multiplied and expanded on the backs of growing suburbs, with new generations moving and forming families, always with a desire to live fulfilled lives in community with others. This, of course, is the lifeblood of church growth. Boomers and the GenXers married a bit later, causing heartburn for church planners. Yet ultimately the patterns held.

In areas where prior generations failed to pave the way for younger believers, new churches were planted. New methods took the place of the old, and congregations unwilling to change were unlikely to survive. The church lived on through the succeeding generations.

Can we take this comforting observation for granted with the millennials?

Put the ten factoids above into your fist like dice, shake them up, and toss them on the table. In the next section, I'll describe what we see laid out.

How It All Shakes Out

- **First, the millennials cannot be ignored in any community.**

It's appropriate to be concerned. Even among the most effective, thriving churches, millennials are underrepresented in comparison to prior generations. We expect a certain age group to vanish from church life for a season, but it's a more pronounced trend today.

Why? Partially due to the delay/deferral mindset that we see in marriage and family formation. We all know that in the past, "marrying and settling down" was strongly linked to church engagement. It's not surprising that as marriage is pushed forward, so is congregational identity.

But we also need to understand that many millennials don't bring the formative church experiences from early life that past generations did. Is that necessarily a negative? No, because the church has a fresh opportunity to paint new images of what it means to follow Christ. No negative baggage has to be overcome.

But we have to tell a better, more captivating story. We can't fail to demonstrate the power of life in Christ, the richness of Christian community.

We find hope in indications that all across racial, language, and educational subgroups, and despite delay/deferral mindsets—millennials still desire marriage and family.

- **Secondly, diversity is now a given.**

Church leaders from previous generations may see cultural diversity as a transition, a new wrinkle of sorts. Millennials see it as the norm. They've grown up with the consistency of diversity in every context—in their pop culture, in their schools, and nearly everywhere else.

What about the suburbs? What about regional pockets of racial or cultural uniformity? We know certain states are still Anglo-dominated, for example, and there are fairly homogeneous ethnic communities. But the world at large is changing, and the change seeps into even these enclaves. Those raised in growing metropolitan regions have been much more likely to have friends, classmates, and co-workers who reflect the mosaic of American life.

Thus, when someone from that generation enters a church unreflective of that diversity, a dissonant chord is struck. For them, this room isn't in keeping with the reality of the world. It's lacking.

Churches haven't been blind to this reality. To their credit, aggressive church leaders have placed more focus on platform visibility and inclusion in developing young leaders. The multisite movement has allowed more flexibility in making inroads to more diverse communities, and studies show that at last, Sunday worship isn't "the most segregated hour of the week," as Dr. King put it, in at least some quarters.

As a white American male, I applaud all this as healthy. But I also respect the heartfelt conversation initiated by some of my friends who gently push back. They feel it's just possible some leaders have special callings to speak to their own communities through their own cultural filters. It can be a language issue, for example, with first-generation immigrant communities, where nurturing cultural traditions is an important virtue. An outreach to a Korean community might be more effective in affirming and acknowledging homeland memories. Is the "melting pot" metaphor the only acceptable congregational model?

My friends from non-Anglo contexts have taught me a great deal about this issue. Some of them are passionate about building diverse churches to reach anyone and everyone in their community. Others feel strong callings to specific cultures or subgroups. Could it be there's a place for both approaches?

On one point we can all agree: There's *no* place for racial discrimination. And while Anglos still hold positions of leverage in our culture, they should be expected to be as open, generous, and willingly diverse as possible as they build their ministries; to "outdo one another in showing honor," as Paul phrases it.

- **Third, the women's leadership issue will not go away.**

This particular controversy has been with us for 30 years, and many readers will have long since addressed it and moved on. They'll ask, "Haven't we already fought that battle?"

Yet even now, it's the elephant in a few church board rooms. I'm not here to challenge anyone's theology or ecclesiology—sincere doctrine is non-negotiable. My point is that the conversation must take place regardless, because of where our people are. Culture has moved on female leadership issues on its own, whether specific churches or denominations have come along or not. Women are heading households and running large businesses.

Conversations on the issue didn't even occur in some conservative congregations four decades ago. As with the diversity conversation, younger generations enter a gathered community of believers and expect, in the natural course of things, to see women at the same levels of leadership as anywhere else. They will ask questions, and answers must be prepared. Conservative theology is as viable as ever; it's simply that it must be adequately defended to those who wonder.

- **Fourth, location is an issue. Intown is in.**
If you're near a major metro, you'll notice that younger and better educated millennials like proximity to the city, or at least to areas of denser population than their grandparents or parents may have sought. Their dream—for now—is not a suburban cul-de-sac.

Will this hold? It's a matter of debate. We know suburban America isn't dying or even ill. As a generation moves toward maturity and family life, green lawns and neighborhood associations may develop the same appeal they've had for the past half-century. Also, with the rise of flexible working arrangements, remote work, and co-working spaces, we could see a revival of the suburban movement.

- **Final point: Kids overrule all other considerations.**
This holds true across wealth, income, and marital designations. Kids come first among the young parents of the moment.

Haven't they always? Prior generations treated their children well; the current one has taken this up two notches. The gear, the experiences, the investment of energy and time—parents are determined to excel at raising their offspring. Churches must show they're as passionate about those children as the parents are.

What's Working?

How are churches leveraging the opportunities opened by these realities? I see several promising developments.

1. Church plants, targeted to and led by millennials.

At first glance, it seems like nothing new. Critics will be quick to recognize the "homogeneous unit" principle from twenty-five years ago rearing its head again.

I would simply acknowledge the inevitable: Leaders are called to reach their own generations. Hearers respond more readily when they identify with the leader. They engage with like-minded presenters; this has always been true. Millennial churches of this type aren't yet nationally prominent, but they're growing in number.

This work's multiplication chapter describes how strong, existing churches are sponsoring these endeavors. So while these may be "millennial churches," their leaders were trained in the larger congregations.

We also see mainline and other groups making their own efforts. They're pioneering "fresh expressions" of new-style groups and congregations. I see these as healthy developments. Over time, any gains may be hard to maintain, but the creativity and new approaches will endure, spreading into other new forms.

2. **Larger churches are using their existing multisite and venue strategies to target this generation.**

There are younger campus pastors, shared teaching teams, and intentional investment into certain key sites with a younger demographic geography. And they're seeing a certain amount of success at reaching and discipling the younger generation. Large suburban churches plant sites in inner-ring and urban neighborhoods. They also encourage those sites to craft their approach to the story of those communities, instead of simply branding based on the sending church. It's an application of the current church planting movement.

3. **Churches are developing programs of training for young leaders.**

In doing so, they retain a greater percentage of young believers by engaging them in the process. This speaks to the desire for mentorship and training that is greatest among the young. Even when the leaders look outside the church for candidates for these programs, they still end up engaging many within their community of faith in the process. These programs aren't easy to pull off; they need sufficient scale and high attention from senior leaders, and they can be expensive. But we'll see more churches launching vision plans focusing on establishing these leadership training programs for young leaders.

4. We're seeing more thoughtfully targeted outreach.

Our engagement section will address this area in more detail. Suffice it to say for now that boomer-led churches are making inroads with multiple approaches geared to reach younger generations. For example, most metro areas have community-wide weeknight, quasi-independent Bible study groups that attract younger people. Wise church leaders see great possibilities there, and they invest in these efforts.

We also see recovery movement evenings that effectively deal with genuine needs, quite often in the millennial age group. Some churches are experimenting with marriage preparation and financial management classes, geared in particular to these groups.

I know of a church that has developed a six-week class for parents expecting their first child—but it's far from the typical "churchy" approach. Three sessions are led by obstetricians, the other three by pediatricians. "Our intent," the organizer tells us, "is to help a parent script the first year of life for the child. We find that millennial parents don't know what to expect. They're worried about messing up, and they need reassurance. By forming them into these groups and demonstrating to them how spiritual development is important, we end up with an attractive tool for reaching them."

I've also noticed serious discipleship programs offered over seven weeks or so. Alpha and Rooted programs, while not designed specifically for millennials, can do a good job engaging them in ways that are "safer" and more information-based than simply being invited to worship. There might be an evening meal, small group discussion, and overnight retreats or Pinnacle-type experiences to build commitment in participants.

One other interesting development: Even as we've seen the decline of gender-focused ministries during the last couple of decades—men's dinners, women's home groups—new gender programing has been tried. A mini-baby boom has made groups for young mothers popular. They can connect, share, support each other, and pray together.

Likewise, short-term, early morning groups for men of all ages have done well in some places— particularly in attracting the younger men.

Don't Forget the Rest

We've given plenty of focus to the millennials. Simply because they're the current crop of young adults, they demand our attention—but not to the exclusion of everyone else. The church exists for all ages and stages.

We're not quite through with the boomers yet. They reinvented young adulthood in America, and now they're doing the same for senior adulthood.

GenXers need attention, too. At long last, with the previous generation finally aging out, their generational heirs are becoming CEOs and political leaders. They're taking leadership positions in American religion and elsewhere.

We know that in America, people tend to receive Christ and form lasting affiliations before they turn 30. So I've focused on these groups as make-or-break targets in bringing the church through each new era. But everyone needs ministry. The best way I can make that point is through a true story.

I'd met a church planter at a gathering where I was speaking, and he contacted me a while later. "I need to thank you," he said.

"Oh? What for?"

"When I met you at the conference, I was complaining about our church plant. It was trying to be young, hip, and relevant to younger generations, but we just seemed to be spinning our wheels. There was no fruit."

"And?"

"You told me to forget about all that. 'If it's not feeling right to you,' you said, 'then look again at your community. Find people who can identify with your own life stage, and build the kind of church you'd like to attend.'"

I smiled. "Did you take my advice?"

"Yes, we did. We thought we were just supposed to do what we saw others doing. But we started a church that felt right for us, and everything took off—we've outgrown our meeting space. We're reaching late boomers. *Who knew* they were being forgotten?"

I need to add that he was in Florida, in a community where people were moving to semi-retire and try new life experiences. A lot of these people weren't seeking a new church as much as fresh connections with people who were doing the same thing they were doing: forge a new life in Florida.

Still, my friend's story is instructive. He was in an environment with its own particulars. His group shifted its emphasis from creating high quality children's ministry experiences to creating relevant youth and service opportunities for mid-range adults. This simply fit their gifts and their capacities. It's important to know who we are and how we're built for ministry, simply than following preset formulas.

33

It's critical that we understand our region, city, or neighborhood as a mission field, in light of national trends. Somewhere in the mesh between general and particular is the task where we're made to shine.

2. The Engagement Front

You moved to a new town. You found your home; you unpacked and settled in. Then you found your new church or religious home.

Remember that era? Seeking a house of worship was immediate business, even for that new family in town who didn't expect to attend regularly. There was a sense of "ought" to religious affiliation that Americans felt. Being part of the social fabric included at least the appearance of church involvement, and people sorted themselves by brand-name denomination: "We're Methodists." "I'm Baptist." "We attend the Presbyterian church." "We're part of the synagogue."

Much of that was an inherited trait, of course. The culture welcomed a broad religious fabric. The town square contained the city hall, the public park, and two or three prominent churches, and it went without saying that you didn't plan certain secular events on Wednesday nights or Sunday mornings.

Some dwell on that nostalgic picture of a supposedly idyllic past and call it *Christendom*—though the reality was that other religious traditions benefited from the high value society placed on faith affiliation.

"Christendom"—the exalted and mostly unchallenged place of religion in cultural life—didn't suddenly collapse in the past few years. It's been over for three decades, whether such was acknowledged or not. Legacy memories, institutional strength, and the last fading vapors of American civil religion have helped keep some traditions alive. Yet it's time to face new realities squarely. Christian belief and traditions, along with other committed religious faiths, have been deserted by the central thrust of mainstream culture.

Call it "post-Christendom," the postmodern shift, a post-Obergefell shift, or any other label. We'll leave the whys and wherefores to others.

What matters more is what we do when we find ourselves in a discomforting wilderness. Some want to discuss how we got here. Cooler heads will persuade us to use our energy in deciding where we should be going.

Keep Calm and Ignore the Hype

Religious adherence is measured in a variety of ways.

One is attachment to a religious institution. Researchers add up the numbers: How many are participating weekly?

A second option is through surveys. What beliefs are being reported in that region? How important do the respondents find these beliefs?

A third measuring stick is media reporting. This is the view from the ground level, in which specific groups and gatherings are observed—churches, synagogues, mosques. What are they doing? How are they changing?

Fourth is the combination of perspectives—say, attendance data over against surveys and polling. Respondents are then categorized as a way of understanding the contemporary religious scene.

You might use all four and arrive at different conclusions. For example, an attendance/participation-based conclusion would almost have to be gloomy at this point, if we look at trends over the past few decades. The second option, surveys, would offer a more complicated picture. The third way is subjective: media reporting tends to rest upon observer bias. Did the editors spotlight an aging, historic congregation, preparing to shut its doors—or a vibrant new church plant a few blocks away, filled with younger people? Based on reporting, is the church all about scandal, or is it known for feeding the hungry?

You won't be surprised to find that I gravitate to option #4, which is more complicated but involves cross-checking and nuance. But it's true that any method we choose involves bias and limitations. We're attempting to quantify a dynamic, fluid, and sometimes nebulous scene involving the invisible world of faith in its many expressions.

Let me confess here that I identify as an evangelical. My biases can be judged accordingly. Along those lines, I would suggest that the word *evangelical* is utterly loaded today, the source of notable confusion in virtually all media, popular and academic. Who exactly is an evangelical? Does the term retain any meaning at all?

There's a popular conception of this word as signifying a certain mix of American civil religion and political conservatism. Yet a recent study suggested that political polls pick up many respondents with no meaningful connection to a church or religious body; they call themselves evangelical because it's a handy label. So the term comes to mean *white, Christian, Republican.* And the more the term is tossed about with these assumptions, the more the definition calcifies.

Obviously, that's a problematic development that leads to wildly incorrect conclusions.[1] This controversy and others tend to support the view that American religion has somehow gone off the rails and may even be headed the way of the Western Europe church.

Yet there are also researchers, myself included, who look for and find rays of hope. As students of two millennia of Christian history, we know that leaders make a resounding difference. Like Martin Luther or the preachers who sparked the Great Awakenings, individuals can change the tide of religious and cultural history.

---

[1] For a full discussion, see Dr. Ed Stetzer's analysis describing a behavior-vs.-belief view of what constitutes the label. https://www.nae.net/defining-evangelicals-research/

My point of view is that American religion is probably stronger than you think. If I'm biased in its favor, it's equally true that many of these decline-and-fall narratives are driven by groups and individuals just as biased in the opposing direction. It's beyond question that some of our cultural narrators are something much less than cheerleaders for a thriving Christianity.

Some of the "church is dead" volleys are even "friendly fire," coming from Christian leaders who are branding their ministries as cities on a hill, gleaming against the sad, gray backdrop of a Christianity in decline.

Having said all this, and having counseled the reader not to panic, we still need to extrapolate some general trends in the Christian sector of the religious economy.

- **Attendance in many denominations is declining.** This is especially true in mainline churches, but also increasingly true in some evangelical traditions.

- **The faith of the younger generations is tenuous compared to previous generations.** See the earlier chapter on demography.

- **Attendance in certain prominent congregations has declined due to crisis, retirements, and other factors.**

- **Attendance aside, church leaders have noted the declines in participation by some of their core attenders.** To read more about that, see *The Big Shift* from my friends at Generis.[2]

Even with all these factors, I still see a glass half-full. My ministry career for the past quarter century has focused on the growing, vital, and alive segments of congregations, church planting networks, and those leaders seeing fruitful results to their labors. I work with their congregations, where people are consistently finding and following Jesus. It's hard to become despondent when you see what I see.

So how can we summarize the current scene? *Nominal* Christianity is dying. *Faithful* Christians are still faithful to attend, pray, serve their neighbors, and accept the Bible as wholly true, and in the same numbers as prior generations.

What is changing is those who were seen as culturally Christian on the outside are now rejecting the label, or living as though Christianity has no impact on their lives.

---

[2] https://generis.com/the-big-shift

Does Attendance Matter?

In the past, church-watchers focused on attendance. It's easy to count heads and keep records. My mentor Lyle Schaller always took pains to create attendance surveys that counted the number of unique noses served every month. That's a better number but still imperfect. Imperfect numbers do give guidance, though.

If we measure attendance, we're getting a partial measure of engagement—which is the new front. If attendance declines, the real issue is that they're not involved. Our worship and activities aren't engaging them. If we were, then attendance, giving, serving, and sharing would reflect it. These are measures of engagement.

But what about some new factors as well? For the first time, we can talk about online participation, how people are "aligning" with us based on their energy, and alignment through some of the previously mentioned factors.

We know we have many people within our communities of faith who identify with our mission, cause and direction. Many even support us financially. They may serve, but not necessarily in our church outreach. What do we do with that?

It means we must add new and accurate measurements for engagement. Those who continue to chase the rollercoaster of emotions related to attendance will go insane—and miss the key factors.

By the way, we're discussing shifts that are being seen not just in churches, but in many other spheres of life. Sports teams, recreation centers, retail, schools, and even grocery stores are coping with the same challenges. That's a longer discussion, but for now, the point is that we have options for gaining clues in how to respond. How are shopping malls or struggling gymnasiums responding in their desperate needs to engage constituencies? What can we apply to our particular world?

The Big Shift is Met by the Big Transition

We've discussed the post-Christendom scene. The shift to the world as a mission zone rather than a welcoming home field has taken place over thirty years, and at least in three ways.

Culture: Let's say it this way. Community culture is out of sync with church culture in many communities. There's a tension that wasn't present in the past.
Leaders: Roles, forms, and norms have changed over these past 30 years—across the board, and not just in churches. Leadership is always a key focus, but styles and approaches have greatly changed.

Congregations and their forms: There will always be a place for new, innovative approaches to congregational communities of faith. I track many of them from micro forms to macro movements. For the purposes of this booklet and the rest of this chapter, I'll focus on more traditional forms that gather for regular worship and nurturing.

Here's what I think we can say:

In their hearts, people still feel a Godward tug. We hear the statement "No one wants to go to church anymore," and perhaps there's some element of truth to it. But my contention is that people haven't changed on the inside. They seek meaning, purpose, and something eternal and unchanging to which they can anchor their lives and values. I call it a desire for faith.

What does it all mean for churches and their leaders?

Evangelism

Again, consider the statement, "No one wants to go to church anymore." Now, let's rephrase that idea: "The fields are white unto harvest."

The distinction is that the old, familiar forms may not work, but the old, familiar needs are still out there. The opportunities are greater and more dramatic than ever.

Here are a few:

No Christian memory means less baggage; fewer obstacles to overcome. International missionaries have always known this. As cultural and Christian memory is fading in our culture, it means we have new opportunities to narrate the old gospel to new generations, and in new ways. The message is just as old and just as new as ever. We simply have to find the tools of the moment. The next three decades present an opportunity and challenge for those willing to be creative in evangelizing and growing believers to maturity.

Many among us howled when Generation X transitions happened; it seemed that all was lost. Yet creative leaders found opportunities to connect to this generation and effectively communicate the gospel to them.

Campuses tend to be good leading indicators of where we're heading. I stand continually amazed at how fruitfully churches are planting among college campuses. Church planting happens in a host of communities (see the multiplication chapter). But I can't help but be optimistic as I see these churches planted on or beside college campuses, raising up leaders for the future.

There's also radical hospitality and micro movements to consider. Most of these I see as expressions of currently gathered churches who help these churches weave into the social fabric of their communities in new ways. David Brooks of the New York Times recently described it in his column, "A Nation of Weavers." He described his endeavor known as Weave: The Social Fabric Project.

Culture changes when a small group of people, often on the margins of society, finds a better way to live, and other people begin to copy them. These Weavers have found a better way to live. We at Weave—and all of us—need to illuminate their example, synthesize their values so we understand what it means to be a relationalist and not an individualist. We need to create hubs where these decentralized networks can come together for solidarity and support. We need to create a shared Weaver identity.

Mind you, Brooks is a Jewish man with a heart for believers. But when I see developments such as the Little Library movement, the Little Food Pantry movement, or the groups that fund small food pantries in schools, I realize this is our cue. Churches can empower believers to weave and repair our world.

Add to that intentionally leading innovations such as the Backpack Blessings movement and the Turquoise Table movement that grew out of churches, and the possibilities begin to seem endless.

By the way, if you'd like to read a special paper focused on these, for descriptions and links write me at **dave.travis@generis.com**.

Discipling in Generosity

This next category could sound self-serving, since our firm focuses many of its consulting practices on helping churches with God-inspired generosity. My practice is not in that field, however, and these are paragraphs I'd write regardless of any relationship I might have with the firm.

The church needs to lead the charge in battling our country's No. 1 idol: the love of money. Does that Goliath seem too imposing? The stones in our sling are all about discipling people to be generous in all things, including money. This takes constant, ongoing confrontation of the sins that beset us when it comes to money and its handling. The American obsession with money cuts deeply, and our teaching of the gospel response must sink deeper still.

Are you familiar with the FIRE movement? This stands for Financial Independence/Retire Early. For many younger generations, this idea—promising and virtuous in itself—could and sometimes does become an unhealthy obsession. It mistranslates as, "I need to accumulate massively now, so I can take it easy in my mansion later."

Needless to say, I have no problems with the idea of saving liberally and living modestly. But like anything else, it can become a false god and a soul-consuming one.

Discipleship in generosity is the counter-culture antidote that drives people to put their trust not in their money and possessions, but in God alone.

You're likely quick to agree—but how is your church doing on the path of transforming its people toward generous spirituality?

Remarkably, this is also a good outreach opportunity for many churches. Younger generations realize they haven't been wisely raised and trained when it comes to handling money in general. There will always be new tools, apps, radio programs, and the like to attract and serve the masses, but the great opportunity is with the kind of mentoring and modeling relationships with which a church could excel.

Engagement and Data

Even now, a decade on, we haven't come to terms with the smartphone.

We made its acquaintance in 2007. Could it be so short a time? What did we do with our hands before that? How did we spend our time while waiting for a restaurant table?

Once, science fiction movies depicted such devices. Dick Tracy had a video-phone in his watch. But the most advanced aliens on Star Trek had nothing to compete with the iPhone—they weren't linked to computers across the globe. Nor did they have so many entities furtively collecting personal information on them, presumably. We willingly forfeit great swaths of our privacy in exchange for the convenience of our phones.

There's a growing sense of unease about that, particularly after discovering how even the largest companies might be hacked—or sell your information in places you never dreamed.

We once spoke of married couples who could complete each other's sentences, they knew each other so well. Now my Google search bar does something similar: it autocompletes the search term before I can finish typing it, because it's been watching my web surfing. It may know me better than I know myself.

Privacy concerns aside, the point is that data collection is powerful today. Consumer behavior and preferences can be measured simply by observation over time. Direct mail companies once used subscriber lists to target various advertising to potential customers. If you subscribed to a magazine for cat owners, that information was worth something to someone.

Now, however, much deeper dives into your psyche are possible. The information out there includes basic demographics, past purchases, and browsing interests. When these are indexed together, someone is on the way to predicting how you might vote or what book you might read next. Scoring systems are used to rank your likelihood as a buyer or contributor or supporter of some type.

Certainly, we've heard about micro-targeting in political campaigns. Some of these principles are being piloted now in churches. Data tools are used to attract, get, keep, grow, and multiply people not just through digital marketing, but face-to-face. Properly used, some of these imposing tools can actually be used by one person or organization to minister to another.

Leadership Network has been working with more than 100 churches to properly understand the data and apply it to their work in their communities. We're not even counting the work done by parachurch and other groups through Web-enabled broad-base outreach beyond local communities. For example, Global Media Outreach enables thousands of volunteer missionaries to reach people around the world.

American churches are using these tools for new insights and understandings of outreach and growth through new tech. We can quickly find out who currently is part of a church and who is not. (In the past, churches set out on foot, canvassing neighborhoods to discover level of interest for a new congregation.) Data points to who might be a seeker or studier, who might be a marriage mentor or other leader, and many other factors. Community needs can come into sharper focus through data use. Membership needs may come to light.

A few examples:

- Several churches have used the tools to target disconnected people in a community. Invitations could then be given for the launch of a new multisite campus or church plant. Several started with over 1,000 in attendance. How is this different from direct mail drops? Those most likely disconnected to a church could be quickly isolated. Direct mail, of course, can quickly become very expensive.

- Churches have used it to encourage their attenders and online participants to join either a live or online small group.

- Some have used the leader scores to qualify who in their church should be encouraged more to join leadership development processes.

- A whole group of churches used it to encourage certain groups of people to be a part of a "healthy relationship series" within their congregation. These messages even targeted digital ads based on that person's likely current view of relationships, using images and words more likely to connect with them. In the past, one more generic ad might have served for all.

These are merely a few of the ways churches are experimenting with the tools.

It sounds like a heavy lift; in many ways, it is. These techniques go beyond Facebook ads and similar calls to action. The good news, at least for many larger churches, is that you not reinvent the wheel yourself. The experts are among us. In large churches, at least, there are likely to be lay people who do this kind of thing for a living. They're waiting to be asked to step up and help your church join the data revolution.

Leadership Network is helping churches properly understand and use the tools. Follow those efforts at **www.leadnet.org**. Generis has partnered with **Gloo** to develop analytic tools which help churches assess their capacity for greater generosity. Imagine how useful it would be to better understand what's consistently true about your top givers or your lapsed givers. Church leaders have struggled to learn more about these key engagement markers for years. We now live in an era where the technology exists to make it possible. Just email me to get hooked up to the right people to help serve your church.

I predict a lot more of this in the coming years, and as techniques improve, they'll trickle down to smaller churches. The costs, while reasonable now, are not the issue. Good understanding of the proper uses are what is crucial at this stage, and with all the things a small church team has to track, the tools are

51

difficult to harness without a great team of volunteers.

Family

As we've seen, the young people are delaying much of the household formation activities of marriage and children. Some, of course, are parents before marriage. Some begin living as family without either.

We live in several worlds at once here. These worlds include the differences in education, race, culture, and wealth when it comes to family formation.

These are familiar new situations, now commonplace for pastors to encounter. The question is whether we've realized how great the opportunities are for ministry.

First, we have the opportunity to help people get married. This means encouraging marriage preparation among followers of Jesus, and helping guide the unmarried. It's less the traditional offer of hosting weddings, and more about offering helpful resources through special outreach. This is good timing for making contact with those who aren't yet connected to a church.

But if I may speak for a moment as a father of a recent bride, I'll suggest that marriage is big business. Churches often miss an opportunity to participate in a more meaningful way with couples in this season of time. At such a key moment, as they prepare to create a new household, they tend to be more open to receiving guidance. Classes, one-to-one coaching, marriage mentoring, and use of church facilities offer a world of possibilities that should never be overlooked.

Additionally, I see more strong churches hosting mass weddings to help cohabitating couples get counseling, guidance, and even formal clothes and receptions. In my judgment, we win in the eyes of an unbelieving world as we help couples over a significant hurdle.

Second, we can help new parents. As noted, young people today may be confident about many things, but not about the daunting task of raising a child. They bring their questions to an institution they expect must know something on the matter—and churches tend to be resource-rich when it comes to experienced parents.

I've mentioned the experience of a Leadership Network church that recently made its first attempt at digital outreach to expectant parents. They targeted those outside the church for a six-week class led by an ob-gyn doctor and a pediatrician, and the goal was to "help script the first year of their child's life." The church included some soft outreach components to include spiritual formation even in the child's first year.

Both of these two ideas are easily enabled with digital outreach tools that target messages and offered specifically to groups of people with these needs.

Finally, family ministry is on the upswing. Churches have realized we must think holistically for younger generations, in tying together student and children's ministry with adult ministries to make them have an impact throughout the week. Generis now has one of the leaders in this area regularly working with churches to improve their total outreach and nurture of these families. To find out more go to:

generis.com/family-ministry

Groups

As adherents of our faith, we believe life is designed to be lived in community. That's accepted even by introverts like me. We understand the way our gifts combine to make us something greater in unity than we are in isolation.

It's not just a Christian thing, however; it's a human thing. People everywhere seek community for a sense of belonging and the experience of sharing life together. It holds true regardless of age, marital status, wealth, work identity, and any other designation. People find meaning in group affiliation. And as most of us have heard by now, the research consistently indicates that people with strong social connections, including church, live longer, healthier, and more productive lives.

Churches gather in larger groups for worship, and they've sought to offer smaller groups for the needs that can only be met that way. In smaller units, we can challenge each other, meet needs as they arise, enjoy friendship, and hold each other accountable.

Many approaches are being used, from traditional Sunday school on campus to home groups to other options. For the purposes of this booklet, let's focus instead on two factors I expect to be prevalent in the coming years.

- **First, radical hospitality becomes a core value.** Here's what I mean. We have to be willing to be radical in extending ourselves, our homes, and our group life to those who don't yet believe and may never believe or walk with Jesus. This can feel very disruptive in a group. But those who can handle the tension will yield kingdom fruit. This probably means including strugglers with different lifestyles in order to answer their questions, prove we're genuine, and point to a much better way without judgement.

This radical hospitality ethos in smaller groupings is what helps change lives. Recovery movement participants know this instinctively, but now this concept applies to those who see no need for any recovery or repentance at first, but are seeking community.

In essence, the old paradigm was small groups were for discipling insiders; the new paradigm says they're also for evangelizing outsiders.

- **Second, connection to a tribe matters.** Imagine small groups as a squadron, when compared to a division in an army. Your small group or squad is part of something larger, not an island unto itself. One's identity will be shaped not only by Christ and his work, but by the shaping of your small group as potters, and then the larger furnace of the tribe. The emphasis of the church as a whole will be reflected in the various groups.

While I see multiple other themes when it comes to discussing current and future small group approaches, my best recommendation is to connect with many doing serious work to improve and establish their systems.

It takes a while for younger churches to find the right approach in their missional context. It takes even longer for existing churches to adapt and change their small group approaches. My friend Kristin Fry at Generis can give you some help. She has some other resources at: *generis.com/kristin-fry*

Leader Development

Another way churches are helping younger generations find and follow Jesus comes through development of robust leader development programs. In the business and sports worlds, firms struggling to find good leaders have developed extensive programs to find potential leaders as young as adolescence. Church develops offer a parallel.

Often the new leadership programs begin as short-term projects where individuals are invited into deeper levels of training, development, and leadership over time. Parachurch and secular youth organizations have excelled this way in promoting their beliefs and forming leaders at younger ages.

But churches are catching up in developing short term- to longer-term projects and programs to equip people from very young ages to be developed into leaders for kingdom and missionary purposes.

I will admit this is more of a large church phenomena. Churches intentionally develop a pathway that consists of a variety of levels and development processes to equip these individuals.

The huge advantage of starting early is that many churches have more interaction with students than anyone else does, with the exception of schools and parents. The second advantage is that leadership development processes can be used with people at any age, unlike many of the non-church programs which merely target individuals of younger generations.

We have long seen the rise of mid-career persons finding new ways to express their gifts and skills within congregational contexts. In the coming years, expect a spike in retirement-age believers flourishing in kingdom service.

What does it take? Intentionality. If you wait, you will miss out.

My friends at Leadership Network have been working in this area with churches for over a decade. Check out some of their thinking and work here: ***leadnet.org/how-we-help/leadership-development***

3. The Multiplication Movement

One of the driving ideas in church growth today is location, location, location. Nothing new there, right? It's long been a central strategy for church in a mobile America—or of any other organization seeking to expand. You watch where the families are going, and you place your units there.

But the big idea of the last few years is, "What if we could be doing our thing in more places than one? What if we could multiply this experience that is *our* unique kind of experience?"

That was the basis of the multisite trend, so pervasive in recent decades. Churches became aggressive about starting new churches, but using lessons from the franchising concept in the business world: a "branded" church capable of occupying several locations.

Some of the strengths of the old church-planting model could be retained, but central leadership streamlined the process; financial efficiency helped; and the age-old issue of coming up with a dynamic new preacher might, in some cases, be eliminated, because video technology made the central pastor "portable." In the case of a dynamic communicator, people were okay with watching a screen. Though of course, more often than not, live preaching was supplied.

But they have also multiplied teaching teams and campus pastors with a majority of multisite churches now indicating less reliance on video and more on teaching and campus pastors.

Where would church expansion go from here? The answer was, to the idea of multiplication.

The multiplication movement combines the streams of church-starting and the multisite movement. New churches plant more new churches in an orderly but fairly aggressive way, obeying God's command to "be fruitful and multiply." And the word *movement* doesn't so much signify a centralized national trend as a vast network of *movements*—plural—as each originating congregation sees itself as a viral instigator. "My church is a movement."

The church-starting/church planting movement has a long history across the world, but what's happening now is a bit different. Each generation takes the forms of church it inherited, and reinvents them in its own image. Leaders, who know their times, create new forms to address the needs around them.

The multisite movement has sprung up largely in the past two decades, reframing the prior generation's approaches into a playbook of effective practices. Leadership Network surveyed growing churches and found that 60 percent of multisite churches have started their sites since 2010. Craig Groeschel, pastor of Life Church, said in late 2017, "We're in chapter one of this movement."

The first chapter of any book should pull us into the story and make us eager to find out what happens next. The multiplication movement, with its emphasis on action, has us anxious to see how the plot thickens. I see it thickening in several directions.

More Compact Facilities

The early boomer generation planted a wave of seeker-oriented churches, and the impact was powerful. The churches grew massive in short order, massive building structures followed, and what were once church "grounds" became church "campuses," complete with ponds, bookstores, and coffee shops.

When I joined Leadership Network, our clients spoke of dreams of building auditoriums that would seat 3,500 for one large worship service. Fill the building twice in a weekend, and there would be plenty of seats and parking.

Some of the auditoriums—no longer "sanctuaries" but "worship centers"—were larger than that.

But suddenly, at the end of this decade, those ambitions are being regretted. Auditorium size, at some point, locked churches into a lot of programs and philosophies that may no longer fit. A big room needs really big music, for example. What about other kinds of services? Does a half-full auditorium seem like a negative experience, even if there are still 1,000 present?

What about other facilities built to match the big-box auditorium; rooms now empty and unused? These campuses were built for the moment, and it was all exciting. But what happens when the present moment becomes a past that has evolved?

Innovative church pastors today no longer tell me about 3,500-seat dreams. The ideal room most often mentioned would now hold 800-1,200, once again with a building designed to be filled and refilled over a weekend. The dreams extend away from the worship center and outward into the larger community, where new sites and new churches can be started. "Build it and they will come" is giving way to "take your show on the road." Doing church in the various communities opens all kinds of possibilities—ironically, making those congregations a little closer to the neighborhood churches our grandparents used. There's a bit of nostalgia for that experience, or at least a modernized version of it.

In a 2017 report from Leadership Network and Portable Church Industries, 83 percent of pastors under the age of 40 in growing churches reported a future vision to launch a new site or plant a new church in the next few years.

In addition, the current multisite movement— and to some extent the church planting movement—is toward merger and "re-plants." In these models, an existing church facility and often a core group are either adopted or repurposed for a new congregation.

Over one third of multisite congregations begin as the result of a merger. Most of these cases occur when a struggling congregation is adopted by a larger, growing congregation.

In the case of "replants," the primary vision comes from a church starter, planter, or network leader who sees a struggling church, but needs a fresh leadership approach and ministry model. These replants often use valuable land, buildings, and remaining cash to rebuild and reframe new ministry for a new era.

Another factor in the growth of multiplication movement involves suitable meeting spaces for new churches and new sites. In the 2012 edition of this booklet, there was a pending court case threatening the use of public schools as church meeting sites. School lunchrooms and auditoriums, of course, were the go-to venue for fresh new plants. The storm passed; U. S. law has been clarified to allow public facilities to be used for religious purposes. The issue may rear its ugly head again, given the hostility to religion in some quarters today. Local, state, and national moods and policies can change.

Churches continue to seek out alternative spaces in addition to traditional worship space. Theaters, disused urban warehouses, old retail spaces, city-owned auditoriums, and even hospital auditoriums have proved workable and good locations. Several companies, most notably Portable Church

Industries, have found their calling in this era. They help churches plan, acquire, and manage spaces.

Also interesting: Immigrants have gotten into the church-planting practice in a dramatic way. Given historic perspective, it's really nothing new. In the past, families have come to these shores, brought their religious traditions with them, and started churches reminiscent of the homeland. Gradually they've put down firmer roots, evolved, and begun to reach other ethnicities. It's easy to forget that some of today's midsized denominations began life as language-specific groups in the 1800s.

Now we have waves of African Independent churches, Central and South American networks, and Asian missionaries coming to America with the specific intention to plant missionary, reproducing churches. The largest of these groups now have well over 800 churches planted on American soil, primarily reaching first and second-generation heritages from their nations of origin.

We've also seen the advance of Aussie, Kiwi, Irish, and English heritage church planters. They plant branches of the sending churches, or perhaps they establish new congregations to reach the panoply of nations gathering here in the U.S. These groups aren't large in number, but they do tend to have higher profiles in the media than the other immigrant churches.

An Expanded Field of Play

The immediate past generation of church startups focused on the suburbs, and leaders were pointed in that direction. Those were the new neighborhoods, the plush green enclaves where families were springing up after the middle of the twentieth century.

The new wave of the multiplication movement has rapidly changed that equation. In a healthy way, the field of play includes urban, exurban, and rural contexts. This is especially true of multisite churches.

The larger suburban churches, then, are the ones launching these new sites in urban areas, and smaller sites in exurban and rural areas. Leaders always tell me that it was a matter of "following the kids" out of the suburban context and into the contexts they're now choosing as they begin their lives as young adults. Meanwhile, some move away from the cities but desire a relevant contextual experience in other areas. Small towns hold a special appeal for a certain segment of younger people today. In the Leadership Network/Generis Multisite Scorecard report in 2013, half reported campuses in small-town settings.

Both approaches should be missionally-driven to be successful. It's never a simple matter of exporting members from one locale to another. These new sites must be conceived, led, and programmed around the new context, with the guidance of those who understand the gospel story as it relates to that context and the people we wish to reach. Who are the natives or newcomers to this neighborhood? What drives them? What does God have to say to their dreams and anxieties? If we focus on past models, we find ourselves back in the loop of reaching past targets. It's a non-productive strategy.

This is a mobile society. People are relatively quick to change addresses when they perceive a better life somewhere else. In such areas, where trends show population growth, we can build newer churches that last. Those moving there are people in transition. They have pulled up roots; they're seeking new relationships, open to new realities. We know these are the periods when they're most reachable—when we have the most open window to attract, evangelize, and disciple them.

As congregational networks, denominations, and churches begin to support both multisite locations and new church plants in growing areas, they have potential to see great success.

Smaller Churches, Too

Where is it written you have to be a megachurch to plant a new church? More and more, smaller churches are getting into the act, planting and thinking outwardly instead of simply for today.

Of course, if you're a very large church with more than 5,000 in attendance, it's actually becoming *likely* your church is multisite. In the 2017 Outreach magazine list of largest U. S. churches, only four of the top 50 were not multisite. Yet we also see churches intentionally planning new sites to be added, or plants to be launched, in churches as small as 200 in weekly worship. It's a change from the old recipe, when the first order of business was to build up a large single site—*then* engage in multiplication.

Multisite church leaders told researchers in 2015 they were tending to start adding sites when they had at least 1,000 attenders. But they also said, "We should have started sooner." Now they're becoming more aggressive about planting or adding sites almost from the beginning. They themselves are quicker to think outwardly, and newer churches coming behind them are following that trend.

Sometimes we're seeing new plants launched with two sites from day one. Why not?

The Rise of Helper Companies, Agencies and Groups

In the past, denominations were front and center. They were the key source for funding, support, coaching, and help for multiplication movement efforts. They controlled the money, the training systems, the credentials system, and the assessment systems to launch new churches. And in general, they discouraged the multisite model. The denomination was supposed to be the organizing theme, not the individual church brand.

In the mid-1980s, we began to see new parachurch organizations coming online to help plant and coach those who wanted to start new congregations. They didn't come through the denominations, of course, but interfaced directly with the churches and the local leaders for training and equipping. This was only one aspect of the decay of denominational prominence during this period. Mainline groups in particular saw steep drops, and among more conservative believers, non-denominational churches became more attractive than the old brand names.

Then came another twist. Church planting networks began to rise in the mid-1990s and early 2000s. These were collections of churches from similar theological or heritage streams, but independent of denominational systems. They began an unleashing of entrepreneurial energy directed at planting new churches. And these less restricted, less tradition-bound networks were far more open to the launching of new sites by existing churches. They also developed their own equipping systems for site leaders, in conjunction with many of the lead churches in their networks. The networks and associations have become a familiar part of the church landscape.

But the most intriguing (and largely untold) story is about the rise of the helper companies. These were specially designed to come alongside new sites and plants, helping with specific needs.

First came the marketing companies who focused primarily on launching and outreach. These created early direct mail campaigns; now they've moved into the digital frontier for advertising.

Second came portable equipment companies. Somebody recognized the need for sound systems and other necessities that could quickly be moved in and out of weekend sites. As mentioned, Portable Church Industries and several other design firms filled that gap. They continue to provide flexible, modular systems that are life-savers for the set-up and take-down teams.

Third came an even more modern manifestation, the virtual service companies. These provided remote staff across a wide variety of roles, including virtual assistants, CFOs, executive pastors, and others. The genius of this innovation was in efficiency. New churches or sites could share specialized staff between them.

Even as denominations began to struggle, in other words, church leaders were finding new and modern ways to work together. Multiplication is only possible when resources are maximized most efficiently, costs are held down, and personnel are made more available and more accomplished than we'd have expected in the past. These niche services have greased the wheels that make church multiplication a reality.

We should also mention the many new technology tools that have serviced sites and kept them sharp. From document sharing, online meetings, and video software, to the many online services that are free (open source) or almost free, planters and site starters never feel they're working in isolation. There are tools, there are like-minded people, and there are special services for almost any need that might arise.

It's enough to remind us of the first century, when new Roman roads, Greek language and culture, and other innovations came together to allow churches to spread across Asia and Europe in ways that would have been impossible a century earlier. Throughout history, "in the fullness of time," the Holy Spirit brings the right tools and the right people together.

Video, Live, or Some Combination?

A dozen years ago, the question was hotly debated. Will people show up for church and stare at a screen? What if the power goes out? What if the system is on the fritz? Churches are almost synonymous with sound system glitches. "Let's sing one more verse of 'Amazing Grace' while our buddy here tries to jury-rig something."

Yet a few churches made it work—they threw up video screens, opened closed circuit lines, and voila! Instant church. It was assumed by many that this would do the trick in any locale. We all know better now.

The most surprising angle of the video vs. live question isn't even about the multisite movement—it's on the church-planting front. We've seen reports, if not a great number of them, of new church plants using other video messages right from launch. Why?

It could be seen as a healthy way of preparing congregations for team-teaching approaches. Or it could emphasize an area of development where the primary teacher is weaker, less confident, or simply "can't say it as well."

I've yet to see a church launch with *only* video. But I'm sure it's happening out there—perhaps in remote or resort communities. There are exceptions to every rule.

The point is, most churches and sites use live teaching rather than video. But why do so many get the idea it's the other way around? Because media attention falls upon the video-driven church. It's a curiosity that seems interesting to reporters. But it's not typical of the thousands of new site launches that are occurring.

Newer plants feel the need to be more intimate, personal. The larger a church becomes, the more likely it is to use video as the primary teaching/preaching delivery method. After all, there are advantages. The message is polished and high quality, from a proven communicator, and that fills one great need for new sites. If a church also uses good team-teaching approaches, it can be quite sustainable.

My personal take: In the long term, this method may wear out. A wiser approach is a multigenerational teaching team, whether live or on screen.

Scale of Multisite

Those associated with church growth have always spoken of certain benchmarks—the obvious "round" numbers such as 100 or 1,000 in attendance, for example.

Recently, 350 has become something of a "magic number." As churches pass that benchmark in average attendance, it feels like the right time to consider multisite approaches and/or planting. Leaders are beginning to feel a certain stability; financial resources may be solid enough to begin looking outward; and at some point, meeting space has maxed out.

For example, let's examine things from the multisite perspective. In 1998, when Leadership Network began tracking the movement, there were around 100 churches using the multisite model. In 2013, a Duke University study reported 8,000 such congregations in the U. S. The Duke study used a broader definition. It included churches with multiple language congregations in one building, or multiple meeting locations at one site.

Leadership Network's estimate is closer to *65,000* or so multi-location churches.

But different scale, scope, and geographic reach call for different standards for implementation and oversight. Take a look at this chart below. The boxes relate to how one conceptualizes, frames, staffs, grows, manages, and oversees a congregation in the area of multisite growth.

A Provisional Understanding

	Decentralized Governance/ Decisions	Centralized Governance/ Decisions
HIGH Scale/ Scope Size	Most rapidly reproducing simple systems	Many large, well-known churches are here
LOW Scale/ Scope Size	A few of the mergers between multisites	Most 2-3 site churches are here

The axes in the boxes indicate centralized decision structures in the church. The scale/scope axis is based on how many sites a church has, and how geographically spread they are.

What the table shows is that, in some cases, the smaller units, simpler in approach, can move to high scale and scope quickly if we measure by geographic reach. These approaches are more "movement-like," with only light accountability and the sharing of more values-based philosophies instead of governance decisions.

The bottom right quadrant is much more typical, and the fastest-growing sector: two to three sites, closer together, with centralized governing. Basically, these are those churches that have started a second site in the last five years, and are planning more in the coming years.

Many times the churches mentioned in the media—those past 10,000 in attendance and mostly using video teaching—are in the top right box. The management and issues these churches have to regularly address look different from those in the bottom right box. It's simply counterproductive to try applying those same techniques to churches in the other boxes.

Likewise, as a church adds sites, geographic reach, or other factors, it must rethink its ministry guidance models to adjust to new realities. The church is now something entirely different; old rules no longer apply.

What does all this mean for church leaders?

1. If you're a growing church, the multisite decision deserves consideration.

2. If you're a growing church, then *regardless* of your multisite status, you should give strong consideration to a church-starting program. Just

over half of multisite churches *also* have a church-planting program.

3. Multisite congregations, the predominant number of which are also multi-location, need to place themselves in one of the boxes above and constantly be adjusting their approaches to fit not only where they are now, but where they intend to go with their approach.

4. Finding the "next site" that fits your particular approach, people group, ministry model, and resources should always be on your radar.

For any number of reasons, the multisite idea doesn't appeal to every church leader. I'm often asked, "Do I *have* to go multisite?"

Absolutely not. The better question to ask your leadership group is this, however: "Do we have to multiply?"

That moves into the area of first principles— that is, your theology of the church itself. I believe healthy, vital churches should be multiplying, because that's what creates a future for our beliefs, and hope for those whom we've yet to reach for Christ.

Multiplication can happen in a variety of ways. Perhaps for some it will be as sponsor and under another new church plant, in cooperation with others. The idea is constant awareness of the need to reach new people with the gospel, to keep our gaze outside our own little culture and toward the larger culture that is groping in the darkness.

Over my 30 years of serving a wide range of churches, I've seen countless varieties of healthy and vibrant churches. Rarely is one failing to multiply in a significant way.

It's part of our spiritual DNA, of course. Also, as our attenders and members begin to understand what the gospel is all about, they expect to follow all that Jesus said about making new disciples. Their lives have been changed by a church, and it seems logical that new churches or new expressions of this church will change the lives of others. Nothing is more thrilling to our people than being part of that miracle.

What's the alternative? Stagnancy. Disillusionment, inward focus, and the triumph of personal desires rather than those of God.

As I've said in various ways, every church is different. Every leader and every local situation have their own unique fingerprints. Each has its own God-ordained future, too. But certain truths hold, in all times and places. One seems to be that multiplication-focused churches are healthier than inward-focused ones. We want every church to be fruitful and multiply.

4. Five Big Ideas That Matter Right Now

This chapter is about developments that are right on top of us. In the next chapter, we'll peer a bit into the future and speculate on what might be around the next bend.

These, however, are issues and opportunities that you're likely to be dealing with already. The point is to identify them and think about how we should be responding. We can all agree that lots of new things are happening. Nearly every week brings a new question. My initial list contained 25 items that "matter right now."

But that's too much to think about in a booklet this size—at Generis, we'll continue to keep you on top of what's new and confusing. Let's look at five prominent ones and consider what they mean for church leadership. Hashtags are a simple way for us to interact on these particular issues on Twitter—if you so choose. That's one way we can have some back-and-forth on a daily basis.

If you want to see updates on that, just follow my Generis Resources page at:
generis.com/dave-travis

1. #AIVoiceEnabled

Artificial Intelligence is no longer an idea reserved for sci-fi flicks.

That handy Amazon or Google gadget you got for Christmas, and that "assistant" app embedded in your phone? These are ordinary, everyday examples of AI. We simply ask our machines for the weather, a movie time, or to order a new box of laundry detergent—by saying it out loud. Alexa and Siri aren't real people, but they're more polite and helpful than many who are.

Have you considered some of the implications? Our computers are reading patterns across broad data sets to synthesize "intelligence." Voices can be recognized. Requests can be anticipated based on what your machine knows about you. The more users participate, the more questions are asked, the closer it comes to resemble authentic intelligence.

How soon before you ask Siri to psychoanalyze you? Evaluate your spiritual gifts? Tell you whom to vote for? I'm only being half serious, but . . .

Planned Parenthood already has an app called Roo. It delivers sex education on demand for teenagers. Your teenager will be encouraged in school to get this app for his or her phone. It allows the user to ask questions and get responses, based, of course, on the Planned Parenthood view of the world.

Isolated and disconnected people will begin to use apps for guidance or to find potential friends.

British researchers tell us that artificial intelligence can listen to a couple interact for 10 minutes and predict the state of their relationship with just over 79 percent accuracy. Over time, they insist, that percentage will increase. [3]Also in the U. K., voice-enabled apps are being used by local governments to provide services to disabled and elderly residents.[4]

Again, doesn't this also mean there are opportunities for those who follow Jesus? It's under the consideration of visionary leaders even as you read these words. Pastors and churches will use services like these. Technology, of course, is neither good nor evil; it's what we make of it. To paraphrase Luther, why should the devil have all the good apps?

"Alexa, find me a local home Bible study group for people about my age.

2. #ConstantMonitor

We've been video-monitoring our sleeping babies for some time now. Smart door security tells the church secretary who wants to come in. As we all know, crime takes a little more thought with the number of cameras up and down the street.

---

[3] http://www.bbc.com/future/story/20190111-artificial-intelligence-can-predict-a-relationships-future?utm_source=nextdraft&utm_medium=email - accessed 1/14/19

[4] https://www.theguardian.com/society/2019/feb/07/control-life-alexa-role-public-service-chatbots-councils
accessed 2/12/19

With various levels of permissions, parents can monitor children—and vice versa. This will especially be the case in public settings and community facilities such as churches. Parents are traveling with portable units that protect their peace of mind, because they can always see where a child is and who she's with.

New tech can provide a welcome check on negative behavior. Are all these cameras "creepy and intrusive," or are they about safety and security? The answer, of course, is both. It's a tension we simply must live with as the price that comes with the privileges of advance. We can track our children, and that's good. Someone is tracking every preference we express, and that's less good.

Preachers now stand on the podium with the knowledge that someone will extract a few seconds of video, broadcast it without context, and the next thing you know, it's Sunday again and protesters are blocking the doors. Something the youth director said or did ten years ago, at the dawn of social media when she wasn't a believer, will come roaring back to disrupt her ministry. For some angry souls, it's worth processing a whole teaching series on audio or video to rearrange and manipulate a few words and create havoc for the church. It's happened before, and it will happen again.

We'll use these things, and we'll also be aware they can be abused. Leaders should begin thinking now where and when cameras will be placed at church. Extra prayer and thought must go into how the website reads, or what the sermon proclaims. Everything today is public.

"The devil prowls like a roaring lion," but now he carries a camera. We must be vigilant, and also be better at it than he is.

3. #YouTubizationLiveStream

Have you noticed the prominence of video today in— virtually everything? Our eyes now expect a video presentation in just about every activity, whether it's church or shopping for an appliance on Amazon. We no longer pay the flight attendant to demonstrate evacuation procedure, but to turn on the video that does that. No politician would launch a campaign without a well-produced video. Any charitable cause would be foolish to try raising awareness without making an attempt at viral video.

Billions of minutes are deployed every day, simply to influence and to persuade and to direct wide streams of human activity. A presidential candidate livestreamed his trip to the dentist's office. Too much?

Youtubization means using content in multiple ways, such as parsing messages to shareable bites, using video for announcement and info, recording of leadership team messages for private sharing, and the like. I like words and sentences myself, but I'm old school that way; I recognize most people today use their eyes for watching rather than reading. Video is powerful, and we lean on it more and more.

Livestreaming is the real-time broadcast of all sorts of content at the moment it happens—and hopefully with better content than a teeth cleaning. One of the more creative ways I've seen lately was Pastor Bryan Carter of Concord Church in Dallas, who used Instagram live to do an early morning prayer time for three weeks. Every morning he logged on and asked for requests from those tuning into his Instagram. Then he began to pray for needs and concerns as they came in.

He had some preset prayer themes as well. The segments were also posted for later viewing, but the experience of being in the moment of prayer with the pastor during this special season of prayer brought immediacy and intimacy. There was frankly no significant difference from physically being in the room. God has always bound believers together "virtually." We're now learning how to maximize that.

We need more pure brainstorming sessions. What else can we do? How else can we liberate God's Spirit to move more freely among us?

4. #MeTooChurch

Two words exploded across the cultural horizon in 2018, with devastating consequences. *Me Too* was a minefield of accusations, counter-accusations, and furious debate, tripped by a couple of stories that came unpleasantly to light. It was all about sexual harassment, abuse, and old, ignored sins that finally had to be confronted.

The church was not immune. Religious leaders were held accountable, too, and there was even a sub-hashtag: #churchtoo.

All victims deserve justice; churches must be above reproach in policies and behaviors alike. Zero tolerance is necessary for proven misbehavior moving forward; understanding, repentance, and forgiveness for actions in the past. Pastors and church leaders will be held to higher standards, and they'll be in for closer inspections. The reports gathered from those under our care must be reported to local authorities.

This is in no way a defense of past actions, but worth noting. I've seen churches get bad counsel from legal providers and insurers, pushing them toward private settlement and quiet agreements. At the time, it seemed "best for all concerned." In the long run, misbehavior was protected and the problem continued to fester. Reputations can be sacred cows—or more to the point, cash cows—and victims can be brushed aside without compassion.

Churches should still seek legal counsel in dealing with these matters, but divine counsel needs to be the dominant influence. Our conscience as a sacred culture demands righteousness. Our secular culture demands a higher level of transparency. Both demand repentance and transformation.

If churches try to be their own investigators, that should be the purview of proper, objective professionals. The long tail of past action or inaction will continue to follow many churches, institutions, and leaders into the future.

More commonly, we'll deal with attenders who have experienced abuse in other contexts—at home, at school, in the workplace. They've always been among us, but now they'll speak up. We must be wise and thorough in helping them heal—and we must know when to make our reports to the proper authorities and our referrals to the proper professional counselors.

This is another issue that isn't "next." It's here, and our response can't be what it was a decade ago. I would never condone past sinful behavior or board decisions, but I recognize that today we must address these issues head-on, redemptively, and with deep compassion for the victims. Remaining quiet, averting our eyes, or simply telling a victim to be forgiving can't be options.

This is an era of reckoning. People demand justice, and in many cases, they're on firm biblical ground in doing so. I advise churches to be proactive in ministry to past victims, to inform and train themselves in counseling, and to make the acquaintance of the proper authorities they may need to consult.

5. #Instagramification

We figured out Facebook a long time ago—most of us, anyway. Twitter was thrust upon us, and eventually we got the hang of that, as well. Many of us are still coming to grips with Instagram, the photo-sharing and video-sharing social media platform that's even more in-the-moment than YouTube.

Many of our attenders Instagram, or IG, just about every activity. Nearly every movement is documented for the annals of history. Sometimes the cart even comes before the horse, as people take part in activities just to IG them.

What we're learning is that life today is highly visual. People are also very self-directed, and everything is a social activity. "The entrée just arrived. Here it is. What do y'all think—should I eat the broccoli or not?"

Sure, it may inspire a sermon or two on narcissism. That's low-hanging fruit. But we'd be just as wise to light a candle in the darkness—and show the candle on Instagram, with a spiritual thought inspired by it for our followers. As a matter of fact, this isn't just about social media. We need to be thinking visually all the time, because that's how people are reached emotionally today.

We need to use images, video, colors, and all the senses to speak to people. People respond to the visual, and they also remember better that way. Images are seared in our minds. One simple photo of a child's body on a Greek beach, as refugees arrive, raised $40 million for the cause. An early 60s photo of hoses turned on civil rights marchers is said to have pushed through the Voting Rights act.

You're unlikely to be that dramatic, but how would your teaching benefit from better use of visuals? What powerful images would fix your message in everyone's head?

The Word has been made flesh. It has been made verbal. It has been translated. It must also be made visual. Jesus showed his wounds to Thomas, who would have fit so well into this modern world, and said, "Because you have seen, you have believed."

We have to help people see.

5. Over the Far Hills

And so we look around us, see all the changes, and sigh deeply. So much to do. But still we must keep an eye on the horizon. It may seem overwhelming, but we have to be future-oriented even as we take on the challenges of today.

One of my mentors, Peter Drucker, said that predicting the future is a fool's game—but that we can look at "the futurity of present events." By this, he meant "what's happening now in seed form, that could grow and change the landscape."

In the 2012 edition of What's Next, I called this the "Wildcards" section—a longer, highly speculative set of ideas that could impact local congregations. The purpose remains not to be an alarmist, but to be a voice calling for flexibility and preparation. Two of the few constants we can count on are challenges—and opportunities.

No Tax Breaks

At present, churches and pastors enjoy certain U. S. tax provisions. Churches count on them. Mind you, other types of organizations receive some of these treatments—not just the church—but it is we who become the focal point for critics who loudly insist that religious organizations get a "free ride." They call for the end of religious tax exemptions.

Several examples and predictions:

Example 1. Property Tax exemptions: Church land, buildings and other properties aren't generally subject to property taxes as homes or businesses might be. The same is true of a myriad of other non church properties such as nonprofit schools, governmental buildings, nonprofit hospitals, and the like. Often, to attract a new business, corporate headquarters, or even build a large football stadium, these entities are granted "property tax waivers" for certain numbers of years based on the belief that these entities will create positive economic benefits for a community.

But churches, especially larger, prominent churches, have become massive, obvious targets in many communities. Critics want to seek to squeeze tax revenues from them. When a community sees a large building, large parking lots, as well as government personnel directing traffic in and out on a weekend, it's catnip to critics.

Of course, many communities already charge churches and nonprofits for paved parking spaces with "water run-off fees" or similar. If the church operates a parking facility as a business, there are taxes. And churches nearly always pay for traffic control when it's conducted by police or sheriff departments.

But generally, the buildings used are not taxed, especially those used for public worship.

Example 2: Gifts from attenders to the church are not taxed as income by the church. In addition, those gifts are tax-deductible by the giver in most cases.

Churches are corporations—groups of people who act as a single legal entity. For-profit corporations are subject to various taxes. The thinking from critics and some tax code writers is that since churches receive income from the public, they should be taxed like a business.

The other challenge comes in the deductibility of gifts to the church. A wide chorus of critics insists that churches are designed for the benefit of those who are regular attenders; financial gifts are just ways of buying the church's services. "Why should these be tax deductible?" goes the thinking. There is no clear benefit to the larger community, so why not deny tax-deductibility to churches?

We only expect this chorus to become louder, especially as churches hold to teachings that the public doesn't like. "Why should those church people who support/don't support X be immune from taxation?"

Example 3: The pastor's housing allowance. We won't delve into the nuances of the tax situation for pastors; we'll just mention that some housing expenses aren't subject to income taxes, as long as those funds are given to the pastor as housing allowance and not salary. Again, pastors aren't alone in being covered under the tax code here. But they're the most prominent ones.

Media stories often focus on these housing allowance stories when a prominent pastor has a large portion—or even all compensation—designated as housing allowance. Complaints are often filed in court against this provision in the tax code as being unfair to other nonprofit workers.

There are other examples we could name, and these will always make the church subject to protest and calls for tax reform. At present, everything is safe. But what are the implications down the road?

1. We'll rethink massive facility construction. Larger churches are already making this change, building new facilities to turn multiple times a weekend rather than one or two glorious events. Multiple services are now seen as a positive, not a stopgap before bigger and better facilities. If the tax conditions change, this approach will become a necessity. Simply

as a stewardship question, it's something to consider in our long-range planning.

2. Alternatively, we see evidence of churches and businesses beginning to share facilities. The church can use what it needs, when it needs it—without paying for the entire property. Friendly landlords are sought, and churches pay for the privilege of having good facilities and rates much cheaper than building and owning a property. This also allows for more flexibility for the future, a tough lesson learned from the megachurch building boom. New paradigm? Church members establishing firms to build auditoriums, childcare, restaurant, and co-working spaces that are used for worship on weekends while earning a profit on weekdays. Everyone wins. These would be professionally run by companies that know how to operate the various businesses.

3. We also need to be helping church attenders and members understand true stewardship *beyond tax implications*. The advent of the new tax laws in the U. S. have raised the standard deductions for most filers, creating no financial incentive to give more than the usual amounts. Only now, in 2019, are many tax filers realizing that. I continue to believe that core disciples,

given to understand true generosity, will continue to give to their congregation and other causes despite tax implications for them personally. I hope to see church leaders focus on discipling people toward generosity rather than being driven by tax implications.

4. Finally, the tax treatment for housing allowance will be the first to go. This will mean adjustments for pastors and churches. Some churches have the mindset they can pay a pastor less now because of the tax treatment of the housing allowance. This will have to change.

It could also mean more churches going back to building, leasing, or having parsonages and manses, as in times of old—which will only create other tax issues, of course. But it would put pastors on par with other nonprofit leaders such as college presidents and some professors, who receive housing as part of their compensation.

Restricted Access to Public Institutions

More and more, in American culture, we're seeing faith presented as a negative issue, unless it's a very inoffensive and publicly comfortable kind of faith. Openly Christian candidates are questioned about their membership in churches that take certain stances. Or they're challenged on their deeply held religious beliefs that don't fit the current secular conventional wisdom.

We're also seeing some corporations suggesting they'll refuse to hire (or rehire) conservative Christians unless they agree to behave in opposition to their religious beliefs. I'm not just referring to non-discrimination policies in the workplace, policies that everyone should adhere to.

The first battlefront in the future may be churches using public spaces for worship or other activities. Already, some candidates are promising to challenge the longstanding RLUIPA (Religious Land Use and Institutionalized Persons Act) that has protected religious groups of all kinds who wish to use public facilities.

Church plants, and the facilities they need (usually schools) are a clear target. The use of the school will be the battle, but the real agenda will be to keep another church from coming into the neighborhood.

Then other businesses—those that rent sites to churches—will come under fire. If the churches hold views on marriage contrary to public opinion, for example, the church will be seen as malign influence, and there will be motivation to stop it from coming in. Landlords will be pressured to deny or rescind leases to what are called "hate groups"—churches.

Third, we'll see a direct attack on church leaders as promoters of hate because of certain views that are deemed improper and now backed by government policy. As we've mentioned, social media can be used to foment anger and opposition. Churches depend upon YouTube or Facebook to distribute their content, but clips and "evidence" will be culled from those platforms and used to make a case. Will podcasts, sermons, and other versions of teaching be labeled "hate speech," leading to removal and banishment from these systems? In recent months, we've seen tremendous pressure on Facebook and Twitter to remove obvious proponents of what some of us would agree is genuine hate speech—but where will the line be drawn? How far is the line between those clearly spewing racial animus, and those who simply have their traditional stances on marriage or abortion?

The final front could be an ordinary believer who holds views that were in the mainstream within public memory, but are now seen as public threats. It will begin in online forums but move into private conversations between co-workers, neighbors, and even casual conversations in retail spaces.

Look for the pendulum to swing far to one side before it swings back—and that pendulum will bring anger and disruption no matter which way it's moving.

No one enjoys any of this, but it's worth remembering that persecution of the church has always inspired creativity and new approaches. I don't know what form any of it will take. I do know that persecution is happening elsewhere in the world, and believers don't simply survive; they thrive.

Anti-religion creates its own backlash sometimes. Its anger and vehemence actually encourages some to look more deeply into the gospel whose controversy is heating up. And believers learn to rely on their faith and the power of the Spirit, which is always the formula for revival. We've grown up with small-town churches on the public square—quite literally—and may even live to see the most passionate churches go underground. But that's never the end of Christianity. For two thousand years, it's signaled nothing but a new beginning and a fresh reminder of who places rulers, authorities, and principalities in power in the first place.

On both the left and right, political groups have quietly established societies and groups that start in schools, continue in private meetings and retreats, and nurture each other until the time comes to assume positions of power and influence in courts and other governmental roles. It's a work-around, a way of bringing strength and truth from the edges toward the center.

I realize many leaders don't like the idea of retreating to the edges and working from there. They believe that as Americans, the center is their birthright. That's an argument for someone else's booklet. Here we engage things as they are, rather than as we may feel they should be. It simply bears reminder that a great deal of the New Testament is written from the edges—from actual persecution and the real possibility of martyrdom. God makes no assurances for us about the comfort of this world, less still about working through political power. The power he offers us is very different, and it's worth the struggle. It's the power of love, a love so stubborn and resolute that we pray for those who persecute us.

We must learn this new skill of working from the edges. Our brothers and sisters in other lands will have much to teach us in that regard.

What About the Mainline?

We can say several things on this question, none of which are easy.

Some say mainline churches have already disappeared. The doors are still open, for the most part, and the institutional structures still stand. But they can't continue to survive unless the pews are restocked, and the trend of diminishing participation reverses itself. Fewer young people are attending mainline seminary. Births can't come close to catching up with deaths, and new members are scarce. Many individual churches are closing their doors, and they're not being replaced or rebooted or giving way to anything new.

The denominations themselves aren't blind to their plight. There is still some funding, and a few ideas for planting, replanting, and expressing their traditions in new and promising ways. But it's sometimes difficult not to feel it's too little, too late.

Most of the traditional mainline groups are in the process of dividing along the lines of sexual orientation and ethics issues. Nor will the issues go away; there will only be new questions to sort out as sacred and secular become hopelessly tangled concepts, no one being sure where one ends and the other begins. The pattern isn't unlike what happened a century ago, when many conservative groups divided into smaller and smaller units, usually over doctrinal minutiae, until they vanished in a mist of irrelevance.

If it all comes to an end for the mainline groups, when? How much longer? Or will they eventually form new, larger coalitions to sustain themselves for at least a few new decades, hoping for new opportunities to cut through the darkness like the first rays of dawn?

Some commentators feel that evangelicals and independents will find themselves on the same path, just a little bit later in the great scheme of things. Such warning signs as the ones detailed in the section above, about restricted access, might point to hard times.

It comes down to issues of truth and of the genuine presence of God. Where God's Spirit dwells, there is always hope. Where faith persists, and believers double down on it, truth prevails. High-commitment faith drives out low-commitment faith, and then high-commitment faith begins to multiply itself again. Twenty centuries of Christianity have told that story repeatedly.

So it's with a certain apprehension, even a little anxiety, that we continue to ask what's next. We continue to wonder what's around that looming, sharp corner. Christian leadership is not for the faint of heart. But I've been here before, and so have you. In 2012, we asked the question, and in the next section we'll find out where we got it right and where we didn't. I think you'll find the answers instructive.

My point, however, is this: Some things we prepare for well, if we're wise; some we could never anticipate. Either way, we're going to make it, one way or another. We made it here from 2012. I have no doubts that should the Lord tarry, we'll make it to the next milepost and have this same conversation—a little grayer of hair, a little more bruised, but with fresh creativity and victories to share.

We don't know what the future holds, but we know who holds the future. That's what keeps our eyes on the horizon and our hearts committed to obedience to the one who is beyond that bend—who is yesterday, today, and forever.

What's Next 2012
Revisiting Yesterday's Future

Those of us who tell you what's coming should expect to answer whether it came. Fair enough, right?

In case you haven't read the 2012 edition of this work, and you'd like to take a deeper dive, just e-mail me at **dave.travis@generis.com**. It would be my pleasure to send you a copy in digital format.

In that year, I predicted several developments would be on the increase—let's call them "more-ofs," as in, "We'll see more of this in the next few years." All my "more-ofs" proved true, but I politely decline the title of prophet. In keeping with Peter Drucker's dictum, I was merely drawing a straight line representing the "futurity of present events." In other words, this kind of thing is as much about having our eyes open in the moment as anything else.

Let's look at a few of the "more-ofs" that have indeed transpired:

More Megachurches

Leadership Network always had a special interest in these churches that regularly host over 2,000 people in attendance every week; Generis not only serves these, but also many churches of other sizes. The press, of course, pays so much attention to the megachurches, that other church leaders tend to follow along with the trends and ideas they see there.

So have there truly been more megachurches? Yes there are.

The numbers suggest that growth has slowed, but is still rising.

While we believe we have good counts on Anglo, African American, Latino and Asian-led churches, we feel like we may be missing a few other churches led by immigrants. We usually find these through news accounts, where these churches are building new facilities and facing opposition.

More Multisite Churches

This was another "more-of" in the last edition. We saw the trend of churches adding new sites, and felt there would be more of the same. That's definitely been the case—so much so that we've given the trend special focus in a chapter of this new edition of *What's Next,* as we've taken a look at the multiplication movement.

More Internet Campuses

The intriguing idea of Internet campuses was just coming on strong in 2012. Since then, we've seen tremendous growth in the number of these. There's been a larger rise of streaming services, but also some significant retreats by some churches in this arena.

Here's the frame: Some churches were serious about establishing a true "Internet campus," including not only the streaming of the worship experience, but significant teams of hosts to do personal connections during the experience. They also encouraged small group participation online. These net-savvy churches have experienced some real growth of ministry outreach and engagement.

Those have regarded the Internet campus as a true campus with its own identity, and not a supplemental experience. However, a second group has experimented with this approach purely as a supplemental experience. They've livestreamed worship services, and while they may have provided hosts and set up online giving, they've provided fewer options for full, interactive engagement. In this scenario, congregants are more likely to be in jobs that require travel, or they're out of town for the weekend, or perhaps they're "lurkers" who have never been to a live service, but feel safer checking things out from the home computer.

Both approaches—full virtual church and "churchnet lite"—are valid and fruitful. Both make the congregational experience more practical and attractive for unreached people.

The third trend moves in the opposite direction; we've seen the retreat from Internet campus by some churches. We're not talking about those who never started in the first place, but churches who actually invested time and resources in this direction. Mostly they come from that second, supplemental group. They dipped their toes in the water, but found they needed to focus more on in-person attendance. Empty seats were blamed on Internet convenience.

"I think we made it too easy for people to stay home," some told us. "And I like a full room." Is that really different from TV or radio broadcasts, which offer the same stay-at-home possibilities? It's hard for me to see the difference.

This idea is here to stay, as the Internet itself doesn't seem likely to fade in importance. The more it takes over our culture, the more the church will need to wrestle it into some positive application. The key is intentional planning, in the same way as a physical campus. A long wave of development is ahead as churches figure this out.

More Big Boxes

In mid-2018 I took an Interstate, cross-country drive. While I saw some very traditional-looking church buildings from the highway and the access roads, I lost count of the number of converted big box stores, warehouses, and retail spaces I drove by. These are now mainstays of regular worship and ministry, as familiar as the wooden country steeple was a century ago. In my travels around the country, I see more "re-use" and less prior use of buildings.

This is the new "storefront" church of years gone by, when we saw it in urban contexts. A church sees potential in a space that can be converted and used, and they get permission for weekend use. Many of the multisite churches have also utilized these spaces for establishing a new permanent site.

In some areas, municipalities are very supportive of this type of redevelopment of former commercial property. No city or county government desires to see an empty commercial parking lot that must be patrolled and monitored for criminal activity. The "halo" effect of a church is well proven, bringing good economic benefits to a city.

At the same time, there are merchants and municipalities who discourage these uses, due to perceived loss of property tax revenues, with the church removing the property from their tax digest.

The generalized view is that communities growing faster than the national average tend to be more resistant; those that are growing slower or declining tend to be more welcoming.

But the general tenor and reputation of the church's ministry also matters. If the church is seen as a positive contributor to the community—this must be earned, and can't be taken for granted—the proper permits and waivers are easier to come by.

More Second and Third-Tier Cities

The title of this section should not be regarded as a loaded term; it's not meant to denigrate smaller cities in any way. We foresaw the continued spread of contemporary worship in a seeker-sensitive-type model outward from the major cities, and into the lesser dense areas. That has certainly come true. Where major cities may have dozens of these churches, even smaller-population cities and counties now have multiple congregations. In fact, in almost every county across the country there is a church that tends toward a contemporary model or form of ministry. Many times these become the largest or in the top 3 sized churches in that county within five years.

Authenticators

The last edition of *What's Next* mentioned multiple "authenticators" for churches in the coming season. As mentioned above, churches aren't taken for granted as positive to the community. The pastor being a likeable guy isn't enough—what is the church doing to make this a better neighborhood? The final headings in this section examine some of the authenticators we predicted. For the most part, I think they turned out to be significant. Again, I was not a prophet; I simply saw the seeds of a growing trend.

Community Serving

While this authenticator has carried forward through big events and outreach focuses in many churches, my question is whether this is an accelerating trend or simply a stable trend.

The most prominent examples are those churches who launch with an explicit community focus.

They often begin with partnerships with elementary schools built into their DNA from the beginning. Others build brands as Gwinnett Church has done, in the Atlanta area. Gwinnett is the name of the county; the church ties its identity to being "#FORGWINNETT" and reminds their attenders to continuously find ways to serve their community with no expectation of return. Obviously this is a strong authenticator.

The idea is this: If the church wants to save and cure souls, it must earn the right to be heard. It will do so by serving its community and building strong friendships with people, who then might listen to the gospel.

These types of ministries are on a spectrum from one-time outreaches—service weekends, summer camp week for foster kids in the community, the health fair held in conjunction with the local hospital, and the like. They include periodic outreaches such as quarterly fixups and retrofits of the homes of the elderly, park cleanups, public school special event and sports outreach-related functions, and more.

Finally, we have the weekly or regularized ministries such as recovery ministry, backpack blessings with schools, prison and care facility ministries. All of these engage and involve people consistently in serving the community in ways that matter. Of course, this list is the tip of the iceberg—the great thing is that opportunities are infinite.

I find these ministries touch hearts in a powerful way. As a result, they attract generous people who wouldn't ordinarily give to the church. The church's most powerful advertising is the public site of its members in service.

Church Planting

This edition's multiplication chapter covered the topic of planting more fully—bottom line, the wave rolls on. Planting isn't a trend but a full-scale movement. As a matter of fact, the wave may not have crested yet, because of millennials. The point in 2012 and 2019 is that for many believers, the church's drive to multiply is an authenticating mark—it undermines the idea that the church is an insular, self-seeking unit. Starting new sites takes work, risk, and sacrifice. Particularly as the new plants serve their own communities, the public looks on with approval and also sees the church as successful, because it's clearly expanding.

Racial and Ethnic Diversity

Demographics are discussed near the beginning of this edition. The United States continues to grow more diverse in terms of ethnicity, birth country, language and race.

One of the distinctives of diversity is what its name implies—every city has a different level, a different mix. More than ever, diversity has become part of the community's ever-changing story.

Indeed the church is becoming less homogeneous. The most multiracial and diverse congregations tend to have two things in common: First, these churches happen to be in diverse communities. Second, they affirm that fact. They make intentional efforts to become increasingly diverse.

Some could say that the former is a fixed reality, but that's really not true—not in the multisite age. The choices of where to go next allow the church to become more or less diverse. Churches can be intentional based on the communities they target.

Our second factor, intentionality, is often reflected in questions of platform visibility, leadership development, and intentional outreach to other community members.

It's clear that leaders are taking this issue seriously, and they want to "look like their communities" as their communities look more diverse.

A June 2018 study from Baylor University reported 1 in 5 congregations are now multiracial as defined by having worshippers from a non-dominant racial group of at least 20 percent. Catholic parishes, with their strong neighborhood bent, are generally more diverse. In that study, the percentage of attenders that are in a multiracial church rose to 18 percent.

It must be remembered that there are some ethnic, language, and other traditions that are less open to diversity. Some of those are hardcore Anglo churches that are in diverse communities and deny the gospel in this way. In others, the hurdles of language and tribalism are steep for any outsider.

While white pastors lead 70 percent of the multiracial congregations, the fastest growing segment is churches led by black pastors. It rose from 5 percent in 1998 to 17 percent in 2012.

Transparency

I predicted more churches would be more transparent with their financial reports and decision processes. I must say there has only seen a marginal increase. I would label my prediction as hopeful.

While many churches are still publishing their annual reports, and many of these include summary data on finances, they tend to obscure other decisions. Even good churches often fail to make available properly audited financials, even when they do them.

Over the next decade, I predict rough going for churches that persist in obscuring basic financial information and the key decisions made on behalf of the church. It's not governmental oversight that worries me as much as the idea of younger congregants disapproving and leaving the affected church.

Having said that, we have now entered a whole new era when it comes to #metoo and the issues of sexual harassment and misconduct. Even now, churches are often having to account for decisions made by boards twenty years ago. Sadly, many of those decisions were wrong. They often hid crimes and misbehavior by church leaders.

The best prescription is to get the bad news out on the past, take the lumps, change your ways, and set new policies that prevent the behaviors. These policies should guide much clearer decisions by executive staff and boards in the present.

How to Lead a Conversation
Using This Tool

This book isn't designed for private rumination. Like everything about our faith, it exists to be shared. It should be talked over, even argued over with your team. It should cause you to open new doors and begin to entertain new possibilities relating to the unique context of your ministry.

So how can you maximize these pages? Try these on for size:

- Read it a chapter at a time with your staff team and ask yourselves about your very specific applications of the material. Place your zip code on every concept, rather than remaining general. Write your ideas on a big sheet and keep those ideas handy as you work through the chapters.

- Read it a chapter at a time with your board during its regular meeting, or schedule a longer session to review what you've read and learned from the book. Compare their notes to the staff notes.

- Convene some of your key leaders beyond the board, and give them the book to read. Let them comment to you as a group.

- Boil down the combined ideas into three time horizons for your specific situation. List no more than three ideas in each section.

- Out of all that's here—what does your team need to address currently?

- What needs to be in your immediate next-chapter plan?

- What are the longer term ideas you should be addressing at a low level, so you'll be ready and fortified when they're upon us?

- Keep the lists of issues on your regular meeting agendas on a consistent basis, regularly asking: Is it our time to address this, and what are we doing about it?

Help Is Out There

Throughout this booklet, we've tried to list other helpers who can assist you with particularized issues along the way.

I stand ready to help, as well to point you to further resources. Feel free to send along your issue lists with specific questions to **dave.travis@generis.com**, and I will respond with direction and help.

Alternatively, if you want to get regular insight and commentary like this, email me and I'll point you to my regular distribution of leading ideas and directions churches are taking to define their unique *What's Next* Future.

See my resource page at:

generis.com/dave-travis

Thanks and Acknowledgements

I give thanks to God for my colleagues that make this resource possible. Our resource team members like Christy Mora and Steve Caton with Generis.

My colleagues at Leadership Network who have served with me since 1995 have contributed their own insights along the way. My new colleagues at Generis are also an astounding resource for me and this work, but also for churches of all sizes and traditions.

Finally, Rob Suggs has helped me in the last two editions of "What's Next?" in taking my drafts and making them sound 100 times better. We even have an unpublished work we haven't published yet. Find out more at www.robsuggs.com

ABOUT THE AUTHOR:
Dave Travis

Dave is Director of Strategic Counsel to Pastors and Church Boards at Generis. He brings a unique perspective as he has experience from both the church world and the business world.

He earned a Masters of Divinity in Pastoral Ministry from the Southern Baptist Theological Seminary and a B.S. in Management from Georgia Tech. He also did a short course at the Harvard Business School in Strategic Perspectives for Nonprofit Management. He has extensive knowledge working with various churches and pastors from all over the country through Leadership Network.

He helps leaders and churches craft their "What's Next" plan for personal and organizational flourishing. Dave specializes in guiding ministries as they transition to more fruitful next seasons. Whether it's figuring out the specific story God is writing for your church, developing a succession plan, spring boarding your staff to their unique purpose, or launching additional sites to your church; Dave comes alongside to listen, pray, challenge, and guide leaders and their teams.

Dave's biggest interests are reading and southern folk art collecting. He is married to Lynne and they have two adult daughters.

Generis helps churches create a culture of generosity that funds their **God-sized vision.** Merging Biblical principles, best practices and your unique ministry DNA, we help you develop a lasting strategy that inspires people to become passionate givers.

GENEROSITY SOLUTIONS

Capital Campaign
One Fund
Generosity Assessments
Generosity Coaching
Generosity Collectives
and Church Analytics

CHURCH
ANALYTICS

Brought to you by Generis | Powered by gloo

www.generis.com | (800) 233-0561 | @GenerisTeam

EFFECT!VE
MINISTRY

Complexity is a natural by-product of a growing church. Left unchecked, that complexity can create a lid over that growth that becomes very hard to push through. Generis has been helping churches fund their God-inspired visions for the last 30 years, and so often we see that the potential for generosity becomes limited by ministry misalignment and unnecessary complications.

That's why we launched the Effective Ministry Team, a robust group of experienced leaders and practitioners who have navigated the growth challenges within some of America's most influential churches.

They've fought the battles and earned the T-Shirt! They are here to help you navigate the challenges of growth, eliminate confusion, create ministry alignment and achieve Kingdom Impact for the WIN!

WHAT WE DO:
- Family Ministry
- Weekend Experience
- Leadership
- Engagement
- Groups
- Multisite
- Multiplication
- Succession Planning
- What's Next?

Brought to you by Generis®

LEARN MORE AT
EFFECTIVEMINISTRY.COM

gloo

What's Next 2020?

How about a data and analytics platform built from the ground up for people and organizations on a mission to change lives.

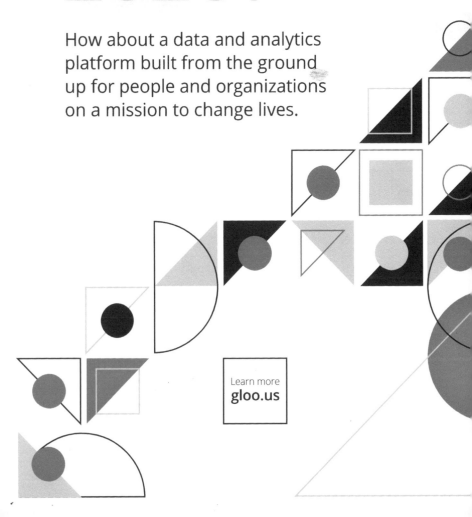

Learn more
gloo.us